# If You Ask A Scientist A Question....

## or, Until You Know Everything, Keep Asking, "Why?"

Book Design by Alex Johnson

ISBN 13
978-1-63132-076-7

ISBN 10
1-63132-076-9

Library of Congress Control Number 2019910819
Library of Congress Cataloging-in-Publication Data is available upon request.

First Edition

Published in the United States of America by ALIVE Book Publishing and
ALIVE Publishing Group, imprints of Advanced Publishing LLC
3200 A Danville Blvd., Suite 204, Alamo, California 94507
alivebookpublishing.com

Printed in the United States of America

10  9  8  7  6  5  4  3  2  1

# If You Ask A Scientist A Question....

## or, Until You Know Everything, Keep Asking, "Why?"

Story by Adrienne H. Small
Illustrations by Tim Blair

ABOOKS
Alive Book Publishing

A simple question asked by a child
illustrates the expansive nature of science
and how the knowledge of
basic science concepts and terms
is used to explain every day phenomena.

"Hmmmm...?"

"Why is the sky BLUE?"

"Ahhh...When we look up, what we call 'the sky' is actually how we see the Atmosphere."

Atmosphere: "The mixture of gasses and particles surrounding a planet."

"Earth, our Planet, is surrounded by the Atmosphere."
Planet: "Any celestial body that revolves around a star."

"Our Planet Earth, plus others,
is part of the Solar System."

Solar System: "The Sun and all the planets, moons,
comets, and asteroids that revolve around it."

"At the center of our Solar System is a Star we call the Sun."

Star: "A massive, luminous ball of plasma."

"The Sun is our major source of Energy."

Energy: "Energy is the capacity to do WORK.
Energy also changes things.
Energy has different forms-
Heat, Sound, Motion, Chemical,
Electrical and Light."

"The Light Energy from the Sun travels through our Solar System to our Planet, Earth."

Light Energy: "Light is a form of electromagnetic radiation that travels in waves."

"Visible Light is the portion of the electromagnetic spectrum that can be seen by the human eye. It is actually made up of all the colors of the rainbow and is called, the Color Spectrum."

Color Spectrum and Visible Light: "The Color Spectrum is the colors the Visible 'White' Light is broken into when it passes through a different medium, like a solid glass prism, liquid water or gasses in an Atmosphere. Each of the colors has a different wavelength."

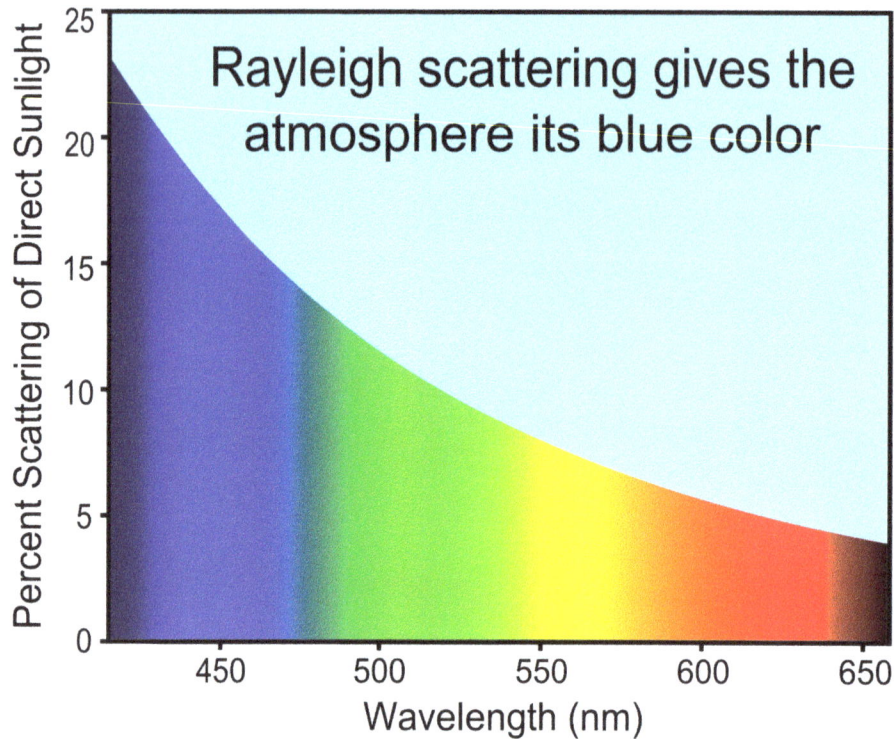

Rayleigh scattering gives the atmosphere its blue color

"When Visible Light enters the Atmosphere, the different colors in the Color Spectrum are scattered. The shortest light wavelengths, violet and blue, are scattered the most. This process is called the Rayleigh Scattering. At sunset, when Visible Light passes through more of our Atmosphere due to the rotation of the Earth affecting the angle of the sun's light, the sky looks orange or red from the longer light wavelengths."

"...and that is why the sky is BLUE!"

"Wow..." says the child,

"So why is the grass GREEN?"

# ABOOKS

ALIVE Book Publishing and ALIVE Publishing Group
are imprints of Advanced Publishing LLC,
3200 A Danville Blvd., Suite 204, Alamo, California 94507

Telephone: 925.837.7303
alivebookpublishing.com

www.ingramcontent.com/pod-product-compliance
Lightning Source LLC
LaVergne TN
LVHW070834080426
835508LV00027B/3449

*9 7 8 1 6 3 1 3 2 0 7 6 7*